Giovanni Cavestri

The Finishing Touch to Fine Cooking

Sauces

Cookery Editor Sonia Allison

Series Editor Wendy Hobson

foulsham

Foreword

Many famous chefs and top-grade cooks believe that, whilst anyone can be taught to cook, the ability to make fine sauces is something with which one has to be born. Although not always the case, a stylish and well turned-out sauce is an indication of the cook's creative talents, skills and artistry.

In this book you w find a good selection recipes and tips – ce tainly enough to give yc an expert start into th world of *haute cuisine*.

Giovanni Cavestri is a 'Grar Maître Diplôme' international sauc maker and proprietor of the ga tronomic restaurant 'Le Corse' ne Frankfurt in Germany.

Contents

Successful Sauces

Ability apart, the success of any sauce is dependent on fresh and prime quality ingredients being used.

Thickening Agents for Sauces

A good thickening agent is a decisive factor in successful sauce-making and there are five basic methods of achieving the characteristic creamy consistency of a quality sauce. In the past, sauces were traditionally thickened with flour and the results were often rather heavy. Nowadays lighter sauces that have been thickened with egg yolks or cream are becoming increasingly popular.

Thickening a Sauce with Butter

Very cold pieces of butter can be added to a hot, concentrated stock and the pan swirled just above the source of heat until the butter melts and the sauce has thickened. Another successful method is to add a *beurre manie* mixture, little by little, and heat the sauce slowly until thickened. The *beurre manie* consists of butter rubbed finely into flour and then kneaded with the fingertips to form a soft paste.

Thickening a Sauce with Egg Yolks

Adding beaten egg yolks to a sauce that has already thickened will give it more body and also enrich and refine it. For 500 ml/18 fl oz/2¼ cups of sauce you will need 1 to 3 egg yolks stirred with 15 ml/1 tbsp of single cream. This is mixed with a small amount of the hot sauce and then the mixture combined with the remaining sauce. Finally, the sauce should be reheated gently until thickened, without allowing it to boil.

Thickening a Sauce with Cream

This method is particularly popular in *nouvelle cuisine*. The richer the cream, the better it will thicken the sauce, so it is best to use double cream. Boil down the sauce over a fairly high heat in order to reduce the water content as much as possible. However, it must not be boiled for too long as it may curdle. Should this happen stir in 15-30 ml/1-2 tbsp of cold water immediately.

Thickening a Sauce with a Purée

This is the 'slimming' method of thickening sauces. Freshly cooked vegetables or fruit should be worked to a purée and mixed with their cooking liquor. A fruit purée sauce is frequently used in desserts.

A Few Tips from the Professionals

No matter how careful you are, accidents can always happen. Here are a few tips on what to do if your sauce goes wrong.

A Burnt Sauce
Strain the sauce into a clean pan but throw it away if the flavour is predominantly burnt. Otherwise reheat it very gently, stirring all the time.

A Fatty Sauce
Leave the sauce to cool and use a ladle to skim off the layer of fat on the top. Repeat the process as often as necessary. If there is very little fat, float a piece of kitchen paper on the top of the sauce for a second until it absorbs the fat droplets.

A Dull-Tasting Sauce
Flavour the sauce with cream, wine or herbs, mustard, Worcestershire sauce or tomato purée.

A Sauce with a Skin on Top
Pass the sauce through a fine sieve into a clean pan and reheat gently before serving. If the sauce is too thick, thin it down with a little milk, stock or water.

A Salty or Peppery Sauce
An over-salted sauce cannot usually be saved. You can try thinning the sauce slightly with water, stock or milk and floating a few slices of uncooked potato on the top. Simmer the sauce gently for 5 minutes then remove the potato. Too much pepper can often be remedied by adding a little soured cream or double cream mixed with a dash of lemon juice.

A Thick Sauce
Cream, soured cream, stock, essence, milk or water can all be used to thin a sauce. A reduced wine liquid also works well. The wine should be boiled down with some finely chopped shallots, a bouquet garni, salt and pepper.

Ingredients

Oils: Good quality oils are the base of many hot and cold sauces. Try to use cold-pressed oils as these are kinder to the digestion and also to the heart.

Butter: This is used as a base for some of the finest and lightest sauces. It can be used to thicken sauces and is particularly good with mildly flavoured fish and meats.

Eggs: Eggs are a basic ingredient of many hot and cold sauces. Egg yolks are used to thicken mayonnaise and hollandaise sauce. Try to use fresh free-range eggs. When cracking a fresh egg on to a saucer, the yolk should be well rounded within the white.

Herbs: Fresh herbs are packed with vitamins and minerals and can also aid digestion. They will lose flavour if cooked for a long time so should be added to a freshly-made sauce at the last minute.

Bouquet Garni: Used extensively in French cooking, a bouquet garni usually consists of oregano, parsley, thyme and bay leaves tied up in a piece of muslin or gauze and added to stock. Other herbs may also be used.

Garlic: This improves the flavour of sauces and adds that final touch. It should be used with care unless making strong Mediterranean garlic sauces.

Wine: A tasty sauce can be made by simply pouring some wine into a pan that has been used to cook meat, and bringing it to the boil. Red wine sauces go well with beef, lamb and game and white wine sauces go with veal, fish and poultry.

Vegetables: Many different vegetables play a part in the preparation of stocks. The most commonly used are carrots, onions and celery.

Lemons. These are not only used for their flavour but also because they make a sauce easily digestible. If you are using lemon peel, try to use unwaxed fruit.

Mushrooms: Use mushrooms to add variety and flavour to sauces. You can make mushroom essence which adds a rich warm colour as well as improving the flavour (see page 10).

Fruit: The best fruit sauces are made by using fresh, unsprayed ripe fruit. It is usually puréed with other ingredients and served with a dessert. Fruit sauces should only be lightly sweetened.

Spirits: Increasingly used in the quest for new variations on sauces, spirits should be used sparingly to avoid drowning the flavour of the sauce.

Stocks and Essences

A stock is made by reducing a liquid and is a basic ingredient of most good sauces. A stock tends to be used when there is no gravy to accompany a meat dish.

Mushroom Essence

Makes 250 ml/8 fl oz/1 cup
Preparation time: 25 mins

250 g/9 oz mushrooms, finely sliced
60 g/1¹/₂ oz/3 tbsp butter
juice of 1 lemon

Cook the mushrooms in a covered pan with the butter and lemon juice for 10 to 15 minutes. Cool and strain. Cover and store in the refrigerator.

> **Gourmet Tip**
> This essence is particularly useful for strengthening the flavour of meat sauces.

Chicken Stock

Makes 2 l/3¹/₂ pts/8¹/₂ cups
Preparation time: 60 mins

1 × 1.5 kg/3 lb chicken
1 medium onion
1 sprig of rosemary
1 large bay leaf
2 cloves garlic, crushed
5 ml/1 tsp peppercorns
300 ml/¹/₂ pt/1¹/₄ cups chicken stock
30 ml/2 tbsp dry sherry
water

1 Cut the chicken into pieces and place in a large pan with all the remaining ingredients.
2 Bring to the boil, skim off the scum as it rises to the top then lower the heat and cover.
3 Simmer for 45 minutes. Remove the chicken to a plate and use as required.
4 Strain the stock into a bowl, cool, then cover and refrigerate for 12 hours. Skim the fat from the top before use.

Variation
To make Veal Stock, replace the chicken with a similar quantity of veal and 2 veal marrow bones. Replace the sherry with white wine and add 4 cloves to the stock.

Fish Stock

Makes 2 l/3¹/₂ pts/8¹/₂ cups
Preparation time: 3¹/₂ hours

2 kg/4¹/₂ lb fish trimmings and bones
2l/3¹/₂ pts/8¹/₂ cups water
25 g/1 oz/2 tbsp butter
2 large onions, cut into rings
1 stick celery, diced
1 tomato, peeled
1 lemon, diced
300 ml/¹/₂ pt/1¹/₄ cups white wine
1 bay leaf
2-3 cloves
a little finely chopped parsley

1 Cover the fish trimmings with the water and bring to the boil. Skim of any scum.
2 Heat the butter and brown the onions, celery and tomato. Add the lemon, wine, herbs and seasoning.
3 Bring to the boil, cover and simmer over a low heat for about 3 hours. Strain the sauce through sieve and leave to cool. Strain again through muslin to ensure that there are no bones.

> **Gourmet Tip**
> Sole trimmings are recommended for this stock as they have a good flavour.

Spanish Sauce

Makes 2 l/3½ pts/8½ cups
Preparation time: 5-6 hours

25 g/*1 oz*/2 tbsp butter for frying
1 kg/*2¼ lb* veal bones, chopped small
1 kg/ *2¼ lb* beef bones, chopped small
250 g/*9 oz* shoulder of veal, cut into large chunks
2 tomatoes, peeled and diced
250 ml/*8 fl oz*/1 cup red wine
2 large onions, roughly chopped
2 large carrots, roughly chopped
1 stick celery, diced
1 leek, finely chopped
1 bouquet garni
water
salt and freshly ground black pepper

1 Heat the butter and fry the bones and meat until browned. Add the tomatoes and stir constantly over a low heat for 5 minutes. Pour in half the wine.

2 Add the vegetables, bouquet garni and remaining wine. Top up with water just to cover the vegetables. Bring to the boil, cover and leave to simmer on a low heat for 4 to 5 hours. Skim off any scum that forms and season to taste with salt and pepper.

3 Pour the sauce through a sieve and leave to cool for about 15 minutes. Carefully remove any scum. Once the sauce has cooled completely, strain it through muslin to ensure it is smooth.

Notes on the Recipes

1 Follow one set of measurements only, do not mix metric and Imperial.
2 Eggs are size 2.
3 Wash fresh produce before preparation.
4 Spoon measurements are level.
5 Adjust seasoning and strongly-flavoured ingredients, such as onions and garlic, to suit your own taste.
6 If you substitute dried for fresh herbs, use only half the amount specified.
7 To deglaze a pan means to pour stock, wine or cream into a pan in which meat has been cooked in order to make a sauce.
8 A roux is a mixture of flour and butter cooked over a very low heat and used as the base for many sauces.
9 Kcal and kJ refer to the whole dish and are approximate.

Hot Sauces

A sauce can add that final touch to roast meat and it can bring out the delicate flavour of vegetables. Although not usually a great feature of a menu, a fine sauce is often the best part of a dish.

Roast Veal with White Sauce, page 14

White Sauce

Makes 1 l/1¾ pts/4¼ cups
Preparation time: 20 mins
1340 kcal/5630 kJ

---

*40 g/1½ **oz**/3 tbsp butter*
*40 g/1½ **oz** shallots, finely chopped*
*50 g/2 **oz**/½ cup plain flour*
*750 ml/1¼ **pts**/3 cups cold chicken stock*
*300 ml/½ **pt**/1¼ cups double cream*
*45 ml/3 **tbsp** dry white wine*
1 bay leaf
*5 ml/1 **tsp** salt*
a pinch of freshly ground white pepper

---

1 Heat the butter and fry the shallots over a moderate heat until translucent. Add the flour and cook, stirring, over a low heat for 3 minutes to make a pale roux.
2 Gradually pour in the stock, whisking all the time to prevent lumps from forming. Bring to the boil then simmer gently, stirring, for about 5 minutes.
3 Stir in the cream and wine and add the bay leaf. Simmer for a further 3 minutes.
4 Sieve and season with salt and pepper.

Photograph opposite (top)

Variation
Brown Sauce can be made simply by allowing the flour to brown while cooking the roux.

Pernod Sauce

Makes 1 l/1¾ pts/4¼ cups
Preparation time: 20 mins
525 kcal/2200 kJ

---

*50 g/2 **oz**/¼ cup butter*
*30 ml/2 **tbsp** finely chopped shallots*
*500 ml/18 fl **oz**/2¼ cups Brown Sauce (see left)*
*30 ml/2 **tbsp** tarragon vinegar*
*30 ml/2 **tbsp** dry white wine*
*60 ml/4 **tbsp** Pernod*
salt and freshly ground white pepper

---

1 Heat the butter and fry the shallots until browned. Add the sauce, tarragon vinegar, wine and liqueur and cook over a low heat for 5 minutes.
2 Season with salt and pepper and serve with lobster or scampi.

Photograph opposite (centre)

Gourmet Tip
If the brown sauce becomes too thin, you can reduce the liquid by boiling or add a little *beurre manie* (see page 6). If the sauce is too thick, add a little cream, soured cream, mushroom essence (see page 10) or reduced wine.

Onion Sauce

Makes 1 l/1¾ pts/4¼ cups
Preparation time: 30 mins
1785 kcal/7470 kJ

---

*300 g/12 **oz** onions, sliced*
*40 g/1 1/2 **oz**/3 tbsp butter*
*1 l /1¾ **pts**/4¼ cups White Sauce (see left)*

---

1 Place the onions in a bowl and pour boiling water over them. Transfer them to a sieve, rinse in cold water and leave to drain. Heat the butter in a pan and cook the onions until translucent.
2 Mix the onions with the white sauce and simmer for a further 15 minutes. Purée the sauce or pass it through a sieve and serve with roast beef or scampi.

Photograph opposite (bottom)

Gourmet Tip
To avoid a skin forming on your sauce, cover it with a sheet of buttered greaseproof paper as soon as it is cooked.

Horseradish Sauce

Serves 4
Preparation time: 20 mins
730 kcal/3055 kJ

---

2 apples, peeled and grated

juice of 1 lemon

500 ml/18 fl oz/2¼ cups White Sauce (page 14)

250 ml/8 fl oz/1 cup dry white wine

15 ml/1 tbsp grated horseradish

a pinch of grated nutmeg

salt and freshly ground white pepper

---

1 Cook the apples with the lemon juice for 2 minutes, pour in the white sauce and wine and leave on a low heat for about 5 minutes, stirring occasionally.
2 Add the horseradish and nutmeg, bring to the boil for a few minutes, stirring, and season to taste with salt and pepper. Serve with beef.

Photograph (top)

Gourmet Tip
A sauce that looks grey or colourless can be brightened up by adding 1 or 2 beaten egg yolks. However, once you have added the eggs, the sauce must not be allowed to boil.

Soured Cream Sauce with Chives

Serves 4
Preparation time: 20 mins
845 kcal/3540 kJ

---

1 large onion, finely chopped

50 g/*2 oz*/¹/₄ cup butter

250 ml/*8 fl oz*/1 cup Fish Stock (page 10)

150 g/*5 oz* natural yoghurt

150 ml/¹/₄ *pt*/²/₃ cup soured cream

1 hard-boiled egg, finely chopped

15 ml/*1 tbsp* dry vermouth

8 tbsp finely chopped fresh chives

---

1 Fry the onion gently in the butter until translucent. Add the fish stock. Stir in the yoghurt and soured cream to make a creamy consistency. Add the egg and vermouth.
2 Bring the sauce back to the boil and mix in the chives. Serve with chicken or baked fish.

Photograph (bottom)

Béchamel Sauce

Makes 1 l/1¾ pts/4¼ cups
Preparation time: 70 mins
1300 kcal/5440 kJ

40 g/*1 1/2 oz* shallots, finely chopped
40 g/*1½ oz/3 tbsp* butter
50 g/*2 oz*½ *cup plain flour*
250 ml/*8 fl oz/1 cup veal stock (page 10)*
500 1 l/*18 fl oz/2¼ cups milk*
250 ml/*8 fl oz/1 cup double cream*
45 ml/*3 tbsp dry white wine*
1 fresh bay leaf
a pinch of freshly ground white pepper
a pinch of nutmeg

Follow the receipe for White Sause on page 14, using veal stock and milk instead of chicken stock.

Photograph opposite (top)

Variations
A Nantua Sauce can be made by adding 50 g/2 oz crab butter and 15 ml/1 tbsp brandy to the béchamel sauce.
A Cardinal Sauce can be made by stirring in 50 g/2 oz lobster butter and 15 ml/1 tbsp brandy.

Butter Sauce

Serves 4-6
Preparation time: 30 mins
1755 kcal/7370 kJ

90 ml/*6 tbsp* dry white wine
1 sprig of tarragon
3 egg yolks
225 g/*8 oz/1 cup butter*
juice of ½ lemon
40 ml/*2½ tbsp hot water*
salt and freshly ground white pepper

1 Boil the white wine and the tarragon until the liquid has reduced to 30 ml/2 tbsp. Remove the tarragon and allow the liquid to cool.
2 Once the liquid is lukewarm, stir in the egg yolks and whisk until foamy. Warm slowly over a low heat and stir in knobs of the butter, one piece at a time. Make sure that the sauce is completely smooth before adding the next piece of butter. The sauce should thicken as the butter is added.
3 Season the sauce with lemon juice, salt and pepper and stir in the hot water to stabilise it. Serve with grilled or poached fish.

Photograph opposite (centre)

Variation
The flavour of this sauce can be varied by using different herbs.

Hollandaise Sauce

Serves 4
Preparation time: 30 min
1390 kcal/5840 kJ

4 egg yolks
5 ml/*1 tsp* white wine vinegar
45 ml/*3 tbsp* water
150 g/*5 oz/*⅔ *cup butter*
½ tsp salt
a pinch of sugar
a pinch of freshly ground white pepper
juice of ½ lemon

1 Whisk the egg yolk with the wine vinegar an water in a small bowl unt frothy. Stand the bowl ove a pan of simmering wate and continue to whisk un the sauce thickens.
2 Melt the butter an when it is lukewarm add to the sauce a spoonful a a time, stirring well. Sea son with salt, peppe sugar and lemon juic and serve with vegetable or poultry.

Photograph opposite (bottom)

Gourmet Tip
Hollandaise Sauce tastes particularly good if a little stiffly whipped cream and a drop of soy sauce are stirred in just before serving.

Béarnaise Sauce

Serves 4
Preparation time: 30 mins
2170 kcal/9115 kJ

---

225 g/*8 oz*/1 cup butter

3 shallots, finely chopped

¹/₂ clove garlic, finely
chopped

45 ml/*3 tbsp* white wine
vinegar

a pinch of chopped fresh
chervil

a pinch of chopped fresh
tarragon

5 ml/*1 tsp* fresh ground
black pepper

4 egg yolks

salt

---

1 Melt 25g/1 oz/2 tbsp of
butter in a saucepan and
add the shallots, garlic
and wine vinegar. Cook
gently for about 10
minutes.
2 Add the herbs, pepper
and egg yolks and trans-
fer to a double saucepan.
Beat the sauce over hot
water until thick and fluffy.
Add the remaining butter,
a tiny piece at a time,
whisking until each piece
has been absorbed and
the sauce has thickened.
Sieve the sauce, season
with salt and keep warm in
the double saucepan.
Serve with fillet of beef or
roast poultry.

Variation
This sauce can be varied
by adding 30 ml/2 tbsp
tomato purée and a little
tabasco sauce.

Gourmet Tip
Be very careful not to
overheat the sauce
at it may curdle.
Should this happen,
the sauce can be
whisked again in a
double saucepan
with 30 ml/2 tbsp
warm water. It is a
good idea to warm
the sauce boat
before serving.

Bolognese Sauce

Serves 4
Preparation time: 1½ hours
2375 kcal/9940 kJ

4 tomatoes, diced

1 × 200 g/*7 oz* can peeled tomatoes

45 ml/*3 tbsp* tomato purée

1 large onion, finely chopped

1 carrot, finely chopped

¼ stick celery, finely chopped

a few celery leaves, finely chopped

2 bay leaves

8 cloves

1 sprig of thyme

1 sprig of tarragon

1 sprig of rosemary

1 clove garlic, crushed

750 g/1½ *lb* mixed beef and veal

100 g/*4 oz* bacon, finely chopped

5 ml/*1 tsp* sugar

1 Bring the tomatoes to the boil with the vegetables and herbs and cook for about 15 minutes, stirring all the time.
2 Work the meat to a fine purée in a food processor and brown in a separate pan with the bacon. Add to the tomato mixture and leave to simmer for 1½ hours, stirring often to prevent sticking. Finally add the sugar.

Photograph opposite (top)

Hermitage Sauce

Serves 4
Preparation time: 50 mins
1325 kcal/5545 kJ

1 clove garlic, roughly chopped

2 shallots, roughly chopped

1 large onion, chopped

3 rashers lean bacon, cubed

15 ml/ 1 tbsp beef stock

45 ml/*3 tbsp* walnut oil

1 sprig of thyme

1 sprig of tarragon

1 bay leaf

salt

2.5 ml/½ *tsp* green peppercorns

1 bottle full-bodied red wine

45 ml/*3 tbsp* whipped cream

1 Cook the garlic, shallots, onion, bacon and beef stock in the oil until the onion is transparent. Lower the heat and add the herbs.
2 Pour in the red wine and cook uncovered, for about 45 minutes. Stir from time to time until the sauce has reduced to half its original quantity. Pass through a fine sieve, reheat and stir in the whipped cream just before serving.

Photograph opposite (centre)

Mexican Sauce

Serves 4
Preparation time: 30 mins
1275 kcal/5335 kJ

1 green pepper, diced

1 red pepper, diced

3 small chilli peppers

1 bunch of chives

1 bunch of parsley

1 sprig of thyme

2 large onions, diced

50 g/*2 oz*/¼ cup butter

45 ml/*3 tbsp* tomato purée

250 ml/*8 fl oz*/1 cup double cream

30 ml/*2 tbsp* lemon juice

5 ml/*1 tsp* tabasco

5 ml/*1 tsp* Worcestershire sauce

salt

a pinch of cayenne pepper

1 Purée the peppers, chilli peppers and herbs in a food processor. Fry the onion gently in the butter until transparent. Add the purée to the onion, bring to the boil and simmer for a few minutes.
2 Stir in the cream and lemon juice. Flavour with tabasco and Worcestershire sauce, season to taste with salt and cayenne pepper and boil for a further 3 minutes.

Photograph opposite (bottom)

Chicken Sauce

Serves 4
Preparation time: 30 mins
910 kcal/3805 kJ

---

*25 g/**1 oz**/2 tbsp butter*

*100 g/**4 oz** mushrooms, sliced*

*250 ml/**8 fl oz**/1 cup chicken stock*

1 red pepper, cut into strips

1 green pepper, cut into strips

1 yellow pepper, cut into strips

*100 ml/**3¹/₂ fl oz** crème fraîche*

2 egg yolks

*30 ml/**2 tbsp** lemon juice*

*30 ml/**2 tbsp** grapefruit juice*

a pinch of cayenne pepper

---

1 Heat the butter in pan, add the mushrooms and stock and cook for about 3 minutes over a low heat. Add the red, green and yellow pepper and simmer for 8 to 10 minutes.
2 Stir in the crème fraîche, egg yolks, lemon and grapefruit juices and cayenne pepper. Cook the sauce over a low heat for about 5 minutes until thickened, stirring frequently.

Photograph (top)

Gourmet Tip
You can also add cooked and diced pieces of chicken to the sauce if desired.

Curry Sauce

Serves 4
Preparation time: 20 mins
579 kcal/2385 kJ

2 large onions, finely chopped
1 clove garlic, finely chopped
2 bay leaves
*15 ml/**1 tbsp** finely chopped fresh basil*
*25 g/**1 oz**/2 tbsp butter*
*250 ml/**8 fl oz**/1 cup veal stock*
*30 ml/**2 tbsp** mild curry powder*
*30 ml/**2 tbsp** grated lemon rind*
*45 ml/**3 tbsp** soured cream*
*5 ml/**1 tsp** sherry*

1 Fry the onions, garlic, bay leaves and basil in the butter for 5 minutes. Pour in the stock.
2 Add the curry powder and lemon rind and boil gently for 5 minutes. Mix in the soured cream and the sherry and stir well. Serve with fish or veal.

Photograph (bottom)

Gourmet Tip
Chicken stock can be used instead of veal. Make sure you use mild curry powder or halve the quantity of curry powder in the recipe.

Roquefort Meat Sauce

Serves 4
Preparation time: 1 hour
1080 kcal/4525 kJ

---

joint roast beef or veal

2 cloves garlic, crushed

1 sprig of rosemary, finely chopped

1 sprig of thyme, finely chopped

salt

45 ml/3 tbsp olive oil

750 g/1 1/2 lb tomatoes, diced

250 ml/8 fl oz/1 cup full-bodied red wine

250 ml/8 fl oz/1 cup soured cream

50 g/2 oz Roquefort cheese

---

1 Whilst the joint is roasting in the oven, mix the garlic, rosemary, thyme, salt and olive oil. Pour this mixture over the joint and return it to the oven. Add the tomatoes to the roasting tin and cook for about 50 minutes. Add a dash of wine every 10 to 15 minutes.
2 When the joint is cooked, pour off the sauce and pass it through a fine sieve. Mix the soured cream with the Roquefort and add it to the sauce, bring to the boil briefly and serve with the meat.

Photograph opposite (top left)

Cocoa Cream Sauce

Serves 4
Preparation time: 30 mins
710 kcal/2970 kJ

---

1 small glass dry white wine

1 large onion, finely chopped

2 bay leaves

6 juniper berries

6 cloves

30 ml/2 tbsp tomato purée

150 ml/1/4 pt/2/3 cup chicken stock

15 ml/1 tbsp water

15 ml/1 tbsp cocoa powder

15 ml/1 tbsp chopped pistachio nuts

a pinch of ground ginger

60 ml/4 tbsp crème fraîche

salt

---

1 Bring the wine to the boil with the onion and herbs and boil steadily until reduced by half. Lower the heat and mix in the tomato purée. Simmer gently for 20 minutes.
2 Stir together the stock, water, cocoa, nuts and ginger. Sieve the sauce into a clean pan and add the cocoa mixture.
3 Heat the sauce slowly until just bubbling. Add the crème fraîche, season to taste with salt and reheat gently without letting the sauce boil. Serve with rabbit.

Photograph opposite (top right)

Pepper Sauce

Serves 4
Preparation time: 20 mins
980 kcal/4100 kJ

---

15 g/1/2 oz/1 tbsp butter

1 clove garlic, finely chopped

25 ml/1 1/2 tbsp medium hot mustard

25 ml/1 1/2 tbsp dry white wine

250 ml/8 fl oz/1 cup well-flavoured beef stock

15 ml/1 tbsp brandy

250 ml/8 fl oz/1 cup double cream

salt and freshly ground white pepper

25 ml/1 1/2 tbsp ground peppercorns

---

1 Heat the butter until light brown, stir in the garlic and mustard then pour in the wine.
2 Bring to the boil, add the stock, brandy and cream and bring back to the boil. Simmer for about 5 minutes. Season with salt and pepper and stir in the peppercorns. Serve with roast beef or duck.

Photograph opposite (bottom)

Caviar Sauce

Serves 4
Preparation time: 20 mins
1770 kcal/7400 kJ

1 shallot finely chopped
50 g/2 oz/¹/₄ cup butter
1 glass dry white wine
30 ml/2 tbsp pineapple juice
salt
a pinch of cayenne pepper
60 ml/4 tbsp crème fraîche or double cream
30 ml/2 tbsp salmon or keta caviar
15 ml/1 tbsp chopped fresh chives

1 Cook the shallot in the butter until transparent, pour in the wine and pineapple juice and bring to the boil.
2 Season the sauce with salt and cayenne pepper and carefully stir in the crème fraîche and caviar. Reheat the sauce but do not allow it to boil. Sprinkle in some very finely chopped chives and serve with braised sole or perch.

Photograph (top)

Fish Sauce

Serves 4
Preparation time: 20 mins
2120 kcal/8900 kJ

225 g/**8 oz**/1 cup butter
15 ml/**1 tbsp** plain flour
60 ml/**4 tbsp** dry white wine
3 egg yolks
3 bay leaves
1 small sprig of thyme
6 cloves
a pinch of sugar
salt and freshly ground white pepper
100 ml/**3**$^1/_2$ **fl oz**/6$^1/_2$ tbsp crème fraîche

1 Heat the butter gently and blend in the flour over a low heat. Stir in the wine, egg yolks and herbs. Bring to the boil, stirring all the time.
2 Pass the sauce through a fine sieve, season to taste with sugar, salt and pepper and stir in the crème fraîche. Reheat gently but do not allow the sauce to boil.

Photograph (bottom)

Gourmet Tip
This sauce is especially good with monkfish. Strips of the fish should first be braised and then cooked for 10 minutes in the sauce. It can also be served with baked monkfish medallions.

Calvados Sauce

Serves 4
Preparation time: 20 mins
820 kcal/3430 kJ

2 apples, diced
25 g/**1 oz**/ 2 tbsp butter .
250 ml/**8 fl oz**/1 cup red wine
1 sprig of rosemary
2 cloves
45 ml/**3 tbsp** calvados
salt and freshly ground black pepper
a little finely chopped mint
60 ml/**4 tbsp** double cream, whipped

1 Brown the apple pieces in the butter, pour in the wine and cook until soft. Add the rosemary, cloves and calvados.
2 Season the sauce with salt, pepper and mint, stir in the stiffly whipped cream and serve with offal.

Photograph opposite (top right)

Almond Sauce

Serves 4
Preparation time: 20 mins
2120 kcal/8865 kJ

50 g/**2 oz**/¼ cup butter
175 g/**6 oz**/¾ cup chopped almonds
1 clove garlic, crushed
30 ml/**2 tbsp** lemon juice
15 ml/**1 tbsp** white vermouth
60 ml/**4 tbsp** strong beef stock or essence

60 ml/**4 tbsp** crème fraîche
salt and freshly ground white pepper
60 ml/**4 tbsp** mushroom stock

1 Melt the butter and brown the almonds and garlic. Add the lemon juice and vermouth.
2 Mix together the stock or essence and the crème fraîche, add to the pan and heat, stirring, without letting the sauce boil. Season with salt and pepper.
3 Flavour with the mushroom stock and serve with roast beef or veal.

Photograph opposite (top left)

Madeira Sauce

Serves 4
Preparation time: 20 mins
1100 kcal/4600 kJ

50 g/**2 oz**/¼ cup butter
500 ml/**18 fl oz**/2¼ cups Spanish Sauce (page 11)
250 ml/**8 fl oz**/1 cup Mushroom Essence (page 10)
15 ml/**1 tbsp** Madeira
150 ml/¼ **pt**/⅔ cup cream

1 Melt the butter in a saucepan and stir in the Spanish Sauce. Boil to reduce the sauce by a third, add the Mushroom Essence and Madeira and

bring to the boil again briefly. Stir in the cream and serve with liver or kidneys.

Photograph (bottom left)

Gourmet Tip
Use double cream for extra richness.

Orange Sauce

Serves 4
Preparation time: 20 mins
580 kcal/2425 kJ

1 large orange
15 ml/½ **oz**/1 tbsp butter
250 ml/**8 fl oz**/1 cup meat stock
15 ml/**1 tbsp** orange marmalade
salt and freshly ground white pepper
150 ml/¼ **pt**/⅔ cup double cream

1 Peel the orange thinly and cut the peel into fine strips. Squeeze the juice from the orange and lightly brown the peel in the butter.
2 Pour in the orange juice and meat stock and bring to the boil. Stir in the marmalade and season to taste with salt and pepper. Add the cream and boil again briefly, Serve with roast duck.

Photograph (bottom right)

31

Sorrel Sauce

Serves 4
Preparation time: 30 mins
1200 kcal/5020 kJ

*250 g/**9 oz** fresh sorrel*	
*50 g/**2 oz**/ ¹/₄ cup butter*	
*250 ml/**8 fl oz**/1 cup Mushroom Essence (page 10)*	
250 ml/8 fl oz/1 cup vegetable stock	
*15 ml/**1 tbsp**/cider vinegar*	
*5 ml/**1 tsp**/ honey*	
*150 ml/¹/₄ **pt**/²/₃ cup Champagne*	
*30 ml/**2 tbsp** crème fraîche*	

1 Wash the sorrel and cook gently in the butter for about 15 minutes. Pour in the Mushroom Essence and quickly bring to the boil. Remove the sorrel and purée in a food processor with the vegetable stock.
2 Bring the vinegar, honey and Champagne to the boil briefly with the purée. Whisk in the crème fraîche, season with salt and pepper and serve with salmon or chicken dishes.

Photograph (top)

> **Gourmet Tip**
> If the sauce is not completely smooth, pass it through a fine sieve or butter muslin.

Scottish Mint Sauce

Serves 4
Preparation time: 40 mins
2590 kcal/10,830 kJ

---

*10 ml/**2 tsp** fresh green peppercorns, ground or chopped*

2 shallots, finely chopped

*15 ml/**1 tbsp** medium or dry sherry*

1 ¹/₂ quantities Hollandaise Sauce (page 18)

*30 ml/**2 tbsp** finely chopped mint leaves*

*30 ml/**2 tbsp** finely chopped lemon balm*

*15 ml/**1 tbsp** peppermint liqueur*

*75 ml/**5 tbsp** crème fraîche*

---

1 Put the peppercorns, shallots and sherry into a saucepan and cook until the mixture is reduced to two-thirds of its original quantity. Pass the mixture through a sieve into the top of a double saucepan and add the Hollandaise Sauce, mint and lemon balm. Fill the bottom of the saucepan with boiling water.

2 Beat together the peppermint liqueur with the crème fraîche. Stir this into the sauce and leave it over the hot water until warm to the touch. Serve with lamb.

Photograph (bottom)

33

Pistachio Sauce

Serves 4
Preparation time: 30 mins
2230 kcal/9325 kJ

2 tomatoes, diced

2 large onions, diced

100 g/**4 oz**/¹/₄ cup butter

1 sprig of thyme finely chopped

750 ml/1¹/₄ **pts**/3 cups chicken stock

250 ml/**8 fl oz**/1 cup soured cream

a pinch of salt

a pinch of grated nutmeg

100 g/**4 oz** chopped pistachio nuts

3 egg yolks

1 Soften the tomatoes and onions gently in the butter. Add the thyme and chicken stock and boil for a few minutes.
2 Mix the sauce with half the cream and season with salt and nutmeg. Stir in the pistachio nuts. Beat the rest of the cream with the egg yolks until frothy and pour into the sauce. Do not allow the sauce to boil, but reheat until warm. Serve with poultry or meat such as veal.

Photograph opposite (top)

Lavender Sauce

Serves 4
Preparation time: 20 mins
550 kcal/2300 kJ

1 clove garlic, crushed

30 ml/**2 tbsp** finely chopped shallots

25 g/**1 oz**/2 tbsp butter

juice of ¹/₂ lemon

10 ml/**2 tbsp** dry white wine

15 ml/**1 tbsp** dried pink lavender flowers

a pinch of salt

a pinch of sugar

a pinch of freshly ground white pepper

150 ml/¹/₄ **pt**/²/₃ cup double cream

1 Fry the garlic and shallots gently in the butter until transparent. Sprinkle over the lemon juice and pour in the wine.
2 Add the lavender flowers, stir well and heat up the sauce. Season to taste with salt and pepper, stir in the cream and bring to the boil. Serve with sole.

Photograph opposite (centre)

Rosehip Sauce

Serves 4
Preparation time: 25 min
960 kcal/4015 kJ

15 ml/**1 tbsp** rum

25 g/**1 oz** raisins

6 juniper berries

225 g/**8 oz** rosehip purée

1 glass port

100 ml/3¹/₂ **fl oz**/6¹/₂ tbsp double cream

15 ml/**1 tbsp** freshly squeezed orange juice

salt and freshly ground white pepper

1 Pour the rum over the raisins and juniper berries, and marinate for about 15 minutes.
2 Meanwhile, mix together the rosehip purée and the port and bring to the boil with the cream. Add the orange juice season with salt and pepper, stir in the marinade and bring to the boil again briefly. Serve with game.

Photograph opposite (bottom)

Cold Sauces

In addition to being wonderful sauces, these recipes make mouthwatering dips for meat and vegetables and can be served as dressings with salads as well as for ice cream or fruit desserts. There are many different kinds to choose from and they are simple to prepare.

Mustard Sauce, page 38

Mustard Sauce

Serves 4
Preparation time: 20 mins
1300 kcal/5440 kJ

4 eggs

100 ml/3¹/₂ fl oz/6¹/₂ tbsp olive oil

45 ml/3 tbsp lemon juice

10 ml/2 tsp gin

salt and freshly ground black pepper

150 ml/¹/₄ pt/²/₃ cup double cream

60 ml/ 4 tbsp Dijon mustard

a pinch of grated horseradish

a little grated lemon rind

1 Hard-boil the eggs and chop coarsely. Mix with the oil, lemon juice and gin. Season to taste with salt and pepper.
2 Whisk the cream with the mustard and horseradish until frothy. Add the egg mixture, stir well and sprinkle the lemon rind over the top. Serve with lobster and scampi.

Photograph page 36

Cumberland Sauce

Serves 4
Preparation time: 20 mins
785 kcal/3280 kJ

1 medium-sized orange

90 ml/6 tbsp dry port

225 g/8 oz redcurrant jelly

5 ml/1 tsp mustard powder

a pinch of finely grated ginger root

a dash of Worcestershire sauce

freshly ground black pepper

1 Wash the orange and peel half very finely. Cut the peel into matchstick strips and squeeze the juice from the orange.
2 Put the orange peel into a small pan with the port and boil over a low heat for about 15 minutes until the peel is soft. Add 30 ml/ 2 tbsp orange juice.
3 Bring the redcurrant jelly to the boil with the remaining ingredients. Allow to cool and mix with the port mixture. Leave covered for about 8 days in the refrigerator. Serve cold with grills and seafood.

Photograph opposite (right)

Provençal Garlic Sauce

Serves 4
Preparation time: 30 min
1980 kcal/8280 kJ

6 cloves garlic, finely chopped

30 ml/2 tbsp chopped sunflower seeds

30 ml/2 tbsp chopped gree olives

90 ml/6 tbsp lightly toastec breadcrumbs

2 egg yolks

250 ml/8 fl oz/1 cup olive c

juice of 2 lemons

salt and freshly ground white pepper

1 Put the garlic, sunflowe seeds and olives in a foc processor. Moisten th crumbs with a little wate and add them to the pro cessor bowl.
2 Add the egg yolks an mix thoroughly, gradual pouring in the olive oil ¿ the same time. Season th sauce with lemon juic salt and pepper. Serv with grilled fish or scamp

Photograph opposite (left)

Mayonnaise

Makes 600 ml/1 pt/2½ cups
Preparation time: 15 mins
4670 kcal/19,540 kJ

---

3 egg yolks

*15 ml/1 **tbsp** vinegar*

salt and freshly ground white pepper

500 ml/18 fl oz/2¼ cups oil

5 ml/ 1 tsp lemon juice

---

1 Place the egg yolks in a bowl and mix well with half the vinegar and salt and pepper. Pour in the oil, a drop at a time, whisking hard all the time.
2 As soon as the mayonnaise emulsifies, and thickens, add the rest of the vinegar and the lemon juice and pour in the rest of the oil in a thin stream, whisking all the time.

Photograph (left)

Quince Mayonnaise

Serves 4
Preparation time: 15 mins
620 kcal/2595 kJ

---

*90 ml/6 **tbsp** mayonnaise*

*60 ml/4 **tbsp** quince purée*

*15 ml/1 **tbsp** quince jelly*

*30 ml/2 **tbsp** lemon juice*

*15 ml/1 **tbsp** finely chopped watercress*

a dash of Worcestershire sauce

a pinch of freshly ground white pepper

salt

---

1 Mix the mayonnaise well with the other ingredients and season to taste with salt and pepper.

Photograph (right)

> **Gourmet Tip**
> The oil and egg yolks should always be at room temperature or the mayonnaise will curdle. If the mayonnaise does curdle, put 30 ml/2 tbsp of boiling water into a glass bowl and add the mayonnaise in drops, stirring constantly. It will keep, covered, in the refrigerator for 2 to 3 weeks.

French Sauce

Serves 4
Preparation time: 30 mins
1795 kcal/7535 kJ

---

5 eggs

15 ml/1 tbsp vinegar

a pinch of salt

10 ml/2 tsp crushed green peppercorns

15 ml/1 tbsp Dijon mustard

15 ml/1 tbsp balsamic vinegar or herb vinegar

120 ml/4 fl oz/¹/₂ cup walnut oil

60 ml/4 tbsp chopped fresh parsley

60 ml/4 tbsp double cream, whipped

---

1 Place 2 eggs in a pan of water with the vinegar. Bring to the boil and boil for 5 minutes.
2 Separate the remaining eggs. Add the egg whites to the pan of boiling water and continue to boil for a further 5 minutes. Drain and place in a bowl of cold water.
3 Mix the remaining egg yolks with salt, peppercorns, mustard and balsamic vinegar. Gradually work in the oil and stir to a creamy consistency with a wooden spoon.
4 Shell the 2 boiled eggs and chop them with the egg whites. Stir these into the sauce with the parsley and cream. Serve with fish or vegetables.

Photograph opposite (top)

Cucumber and Herb Sauce

Serves 4
Preparation time: 15 mins
440 kcal/1840 kJ

---

¹/₂ cucumber

60 ml/4 tbsp double cream

10 ml/2 tsp lemon juice

1 clove garlic, finely chopped

1 onion, finely chopped

10 ml/2 tsp capers, finely chopped

5 ml/1 tsp paprika

a pinch of cayenne pepper

60 ml/ 4 tbsp finely chopped fresh mixed herbs

---

1 Work the cucumber to a purée in a food processor and mix well with the cream, lemon juice, garlic and onion.
2 Season the sauce with the capers, paprika and cayenne pepper and stir in the herbs. Serve with braised fish.

Photograph opposite (centre)

Mixed Salad Sauce

Serves 4
Preparation time: 15 mins
905 kcal/3800 kJ

---

75 ml/5 tbsp olive oil

30 ml/2 tbsp raspberry vinegar

90 ml/6 tbsp white port

salt and freshly ground white pepper

5 ml/1 tsp sugar

4 tomatoes, skinned and deseeded

200 g/7 oz cucumber, thinly sliced

225 g/8 oz mushrooms, quartered

2 hard-boiled eggs, chopped

50 g/2 oz/2 tbsp chopped cress

---

1 Mix together the oil, vinegar and port, add salt, pepper and sugar and stir in the vegetables. Transfer to a bowl.
2 Garnish the sauce with chopped egg and cress

Photograph opposite (bottom)

Frothy Red Wine Sauce

Serves 4
Preparation time: 15 mins
1600 kcal/6680 kJ

8 egg yolks
100 g/**4 oz**/$^1/_2$ cup sugar
45 ml/**3 tbsp** rum
600 ml/**1 pt**/2$^1/_2$ cups red wine

1 Stir the egg yolks, sugar, rum and red wine together. Warm over a low heat, stirring constantly until the sugar melts.
2 Beat until the sauce thickens. Serve hot or cold with ice cream or fruit salad.

Photograph (left)

> **Gourmet Tip**
> If the temperature of a whipped sauce is allowed to get too hot, the sauce may curdle.

Vanilla and Advocaat Cream

Serves 4
Preparation time: 20 mins
960 kcal/4035 kJ

500 ml/*18 fl oz*/2¹/₄ cups milk
a pinch of salt
1 vanilla pod
2 eggs
100 g/*4 oz*/¹/₂ cup caster sugar
5 ml/*1 tsp* cornflour
15 ml/*3 tsp* advocaat

1 Bring the milk, salt and vanilla pod to the boil over a low heat.
2 Beat the eggs and sugar until thick and frothy. Strain the milk into the egg and sugar mixture.
3 Mix the cornflour with the advocaat and add it to the milk. Heat the mixture until it just comes to the boil, stirring continuously. Remove from the heat, pour into a clean bowl and leave to cool completely, stirring frequently.

Photograph (right)

Avocado Sauce

Serves 4
Preparation time: 35 mins
1550 kcal/6480 kJ

---

250 ml/*8 fl oz*/1 cup of milk

150 ml/*¹/₄ pt*/*²/₃ cup double
cream*

75 g/*3 oz*/*¹/₃ cup caster
sugar*

3 egg yolks

2 avocados, puréed

30 ml/*2 tbsp* finely chopped
walnuts

15 ml/*1 tbsp* mint jelly

a pinch of grated nutmeg

---

1 Heat the milk, cream
and sugar over a low heat
until the sugar has com-
pletely dissolved.
2 Beat the egg yolks in a
food processor until fro-
thy. Mix in the avocados,
walnuts, sugar mixture
and mint jelly and stir until
thoroughly mixed. Allow
the sauce to cool and add
a little grated nutmeg.
Serve cold with fruit or
prawns.

*Photograph opposite
(top left)*

Peach Sauce

Serves 4
Preparation time: 15 mins
2100 kcal/8780 kJ

---

15 ml/*1 tbsp* lemon juice

30 ml/*2 tbsp* Grand Marnier

150 g/*5 oz* walnuts

8 ripe, juicy peaches,
peeled and stoned

75 g/*3 oz*/*¹/₃ cup caster
sugar*

30 ml/*2 tbsp* sugar

---

1 Dribble the lemon juice
and Grand Mariner over
the walnuts and leave for
about 10 minutes.
2 Meanwhile, work the
peaches to a purée in a
food processor. Add the
walnut mixture to the
peach purée and stir well
to combine. Serve with
fresh fruit.

*Photograph opposite
(top right)*

Fig Sauce

Serves 4
Preparation time: 10 mins
755 kcal/3160 kJ

3-4 fresh figs, finely
chopped

90 ml/*6 tbsp* sesame oil

30 ml/*2 tbsp* cashew nuts,
chopped

30 ml/*2 tbsp* sultanas,
chopped

a dash of tabasco sauce

15 ml/*1 tbsp* dry vermouth

---

1 Mix the figs well with the
sesame oil.
2 Stir in the remaining ingredients, and serve with
cold meats.

*Photograph opposite
(bottom left)*

Strawberry Sauce

Serves 4
Preparation time: 25 mins
740 kcal/3095 kJ

---

75 g/*3 oz*/*¹/₃ cup caster
sugar*

250 ml/*8 fl oz*/1 cup water

1 small cup coffee

350 g/*12 oz* fresh
strawberries

15 ml/*1 tbsp* advocaat

5 ml/*1 tsp* lemon juice

15 ml/*1 tbsp* raspberry
brandy

---

1 Dissolve the sugar in
the water and coffee over
a low heat. Crush the
strawberries with a fork
and add to coffee mixture
Bring to the boil and simmer gently for 2 to 3
minutes.
2 Pour the sauce into a
clean container and allow
to cool. Stir in the remaining ingredients well and
store in the refrigerator
Serve with ice cream o
sponge puddings.

*Photograph opposite
(bottom right)*

Index of Recipes

foulsham
Yeovil Road, Slough, Berkshire, SL1 4JH

ISBN 0-572-01705-7

This English language edition copyright
© 1992 W. Foulsham & Co. Ltd
Originally published by Falken-Verlag,
GmbH, Niedernhausen TS, Germany
Photographs copyright © Falken-Verlag

Printed in Portugal